NICK NAIRN

# Chicken, Duck and Game

# NICK NAIRN

# Chicken, Duck and Game

*Photography by Philip Wilkins*

WEIDENFELD & NICOLSON

# Nick Nairn

Nick Nairn started his career as a Navigating Officer in the Merchant Navy; as he travelled the world he sampled a huge variety of foods. While on leave, he began cooking for friends and discovered a talent and interest that eventually led, in 1986, to his converting an old mill near Aberfoyle in Scotland into Braeval. Nick's cooking was encouraged and inspired by some of Scotland's best chefs, including David Wilson, Hilary Brown and Betty Allen, and in 1991, at the age of 32, Nick was awarded a Michelin star which he has retained ever since.

Braeval has won many awards, including Macmillan/Decanter Best Restaurant and Scottish Field Restaurant of the Year, and is highly rated in numerous guides, including *Michelin* and *The Good Food Guide*. Nick has also started a cookery school at Braeval and holds many cookery demonstrations – his distinctive style and enthusiasm conveys an informative, entertaining and inspiring experience to his audiences.

Nick has made several television appearances: on *Ready Steady Cook, Food and Drink* and *Who'll Do the Pudding?*, as a guest judge on *Masterchef* and *Junior Masterchef*, and as part of the BBC *Good Food Show*. He is a regular contributor to a number of Radio Scotland programmes. He has presented two of his own cookery series on BBC2 – *Wild Harvest 1* and *2* – and is shortly to present a third; and he is the author of the accompanying best-selling BBC books.

Photograph by Graham Lees

# Contents

DUCK CONFIT
WITH LENTIL AND HERB FETTUCCINE  10

SEARED GARLIC, LEMON AND CHILLI CHICKEN
WITH PARMESAN  12

CHICKEN LIVER AND CHIVE MASH PIES
WITH ONION GRAVY  14

SLOW-ROAST CHICKEN THIGHS
WITH SPICY COUSCOUS AND APRICOT AND MINT SAUCE  16

PAN-FRIED GUINEA FOWL
WITH A MEDITERRANEAN VEGETABLE CRUMBLE  18

PHEASANT BREAST WITH SPINACH,
POTATO PANCAKE AND A MUSHROOM VELOUTÉ SAUCE  20

PIGEON BREASTS WITH ROAST BARLEY,
WILD MUSHROOMS AND SAUCE VIERGE  22

SEARED BREAST OF MALLARD
WITH SAVOURY LENTILS  24

GLAZED DUCK SKEWERS WITH CHINESE GREENS
AND A SOY, HONEY AND GINGER SAUCE  26

ROAST SADDLE OF HARE WITH PARSNIP PURÉE
AND A GAME AND CHOCOLATE SAUCE  28

SLOW-ROAST HAUNCH OF VENISON
WITH RED CABBAGE AND THE BEST-EVER ROAST POTATOES  30

MEDALLIONS OF VENISON
WITH ROASTED ROOT VEGETABLES AND A RICH GAME SAUCE  32


THE BASICS

CHICKEN STOCK  34

BEEF STOCK  34

POTATO PANCAKES  35

BEST-EVER ROAST POTATOES  35

TAPENADE SAUCE  36

RED ONION MARMALADE  37

DEEP-FRIED HERBS  37

There's no big mystery,
it's just food and the simpler
the better.

# Introduction

This book contains just a few of my favourite examples of what you can do with chicken, duck and game. As I believe that the simplest is the best, cooking with these ingredients usually means to me just seasoning and then cooking them as quickly as possible over a high heat. This way, they retain all their characteristic flavours, which can then be complemented by some suitably chosen accompaniments to show them off in the best light.

In Scotland we are lucky to be able to get good chicken, duck and especially game quite readily, but thanks to today's supermarkets and a greater awareness of good food, they are now easily available elsewhere too. Whenever you can, try to use naturally reared, free-range or even 'wild' ingredients, because the flavour will be so much better. No recipe will ever be a complete success unless all the individual ingredients are really good to start with. And try to shop and cook on the same day, choosing what to cook by what looks best at the time.

Some of these recipes may seem to take a little time to prepare, but I hope they will show you what great things you can do with the slightly more unusual ingredients such as hare, pigeon and chicken livers as well as the more usual chicken and duck. I hope you enjoy eating them too!

# DUCK CONFIT
## *with lentil and herb fettuccine*

**SERVES 4**

4 large duck legs
1 whole head of garlic,
    cut in half horizontally
salt and pepper
leaves from 4 sprigs of thyme
4 dried bay leaves, crumbled
duck fat or sunflower oil to cover
225 g/8 oz dried fettuccine
    pasta

**Lentil and herb sauce**

25 g/1 oz unsalted butter
4 shallots or 1 small onion,
    very finely chopped
6 button mushrooms, sliced
½ garlic clove, crushed
1 bay leaf
1 sprig of thyme
4 white peppercorns, crushed
250 ml/8 fl oz dry white wine
450 ml/15 fl oz chicken stock
85 ml/3 fl oz double cream
50 g/2 oz dried Puy lentils
1 tablespoon each of chopped
    fresh chives, parsley
    and tarragon

**To serve**

deep–fried Parma ham (page 37)

The day before, prepare the duck confit. Lay the duck legs in a small roasting tin, rub the garlic over the skin, then sprinkle with plenty of salt and pepper and rub it in well. Tuck the garlic in among the legs and sprinkle over the thyme and bay leaves. Cover with cling film and leave in the refrigerator overnight. The next day, rub the aromatics off the duck and pack into a large saucepan. Cover with duck fat or sunflower oil and bring up to a very gentle simmer. Cook over a very low heat for 2–2½ hours or until very tender.

For the sauce, melt the butter in a saucepan. Add the shallots, mushrooms, garlic, bay leaf, thyme and peppercorns. Fry until golden, then add the wine and boil until reduced to a couple of tablespoons. Add the stock and boil until reduced by two-thirds. Add the cream, bring back to the boil and then strain into a clean saucepan. Check the seasoning and set aside. Simmer the lentils in lightly salted boiling water for about 15 minutes or until tender. Drain and set aside.

Preheat the oven to 220°C/425°F/Gas Mark 7. Lay the duck legs on a rack set over a roasting tin and roast at the top of the oven, turning once or twice, until the skin is crisp and golden. Leave to cool slightly and then remove the meat from the bones and flake it. Cook the pasta in boiling water until al dente. Reheat the sauce and stir in the lentils and the herbs. Drain the pasta and return to the pan. Add the sauce and the duck and toss together over a low heat. Divide between four warmed bowls and top with deep–fried Parma ham.

*Almost a meal in itself, serve a light first course such as a gâteau of roast vegetables with goats' cheese and rocket salad and finish with rich but cool and silky chocolate pots.*

# SEARED GARLIC, LEMON AND CHILLI CHICKEN WITH PARMESAN

**SERVES 4 AS A STARTER**

2 large boneless chicken
  breasts, corn-fed if possible,
  skinned
coarsely grated zest of 1 lemon
2 teaspoons chilli oil
2 teaspoons olive oil
1 garlic clove, very finely chopped
1 red chilli, seeded and very
  finely chopped
salt and pepper
2 tablespoons sunflower oil
juice of ½ lemon
25 g/1 oz Parmesan cheese,
  shaved

**Tomato and chive dressing**
6 tablespoons olive oil
2 tablespoons fresh lemon juice
2 plum tomatoes, skinned,
  seeded and finely diced
1 tablespoon chopped fresh
  chives

**Salad of fresh herbs**
50 g/2 oz sugar snap peas,
  each cut into 3 or 4 pieces
small bunch each of fresh
  flat-leaf parsley, tarragon,
  chives and rocket

Remove the little fillet from the underside of each chicken breast. Cut the breasts into very thin slices and cut each fillet into three. You should end up with about 25–30 pieces of chicken. Mix the lemon zest, chilli oil, olive oil, garlic, red chilli and some salt and pepper in a bowl. Stir in the chicken and leave to marinate for 3–6 hours.

For the tomato and chive dressing, whisk the oil, lemon juice and some seasoning together in a small bowl. Spoon out 2 teaspoons of the mixture and set aside. Stir the diced tomatoes and chives into the remainder.

Heat a frying pan until very hot. Add the sunflower oil and the chicken (in batches if necessary so that you don't overcrowd the pan) and stir-fry over a high heat for a few minutes until well browned. Sprinkle over the lemon juice and some salt and pepper, shake the pan over a high heat for a second or two and then set aside.

To serve, place the sugar snap peas and the mixed fresh herbs in a bowl and toss with the reserved dressing to coat the leaves lightly. Pile into the centre of four large plates. Place the chicken around the edge of the salad and spoon over the tomato and chive dressing. Scatter the Parmesan shavings over the chicken and serve immediately.

*After this vibrant starter, serve a main course of steamed fillet of cod with spinach, chive mashed potatoes and a rich butter sauce, and a passion fruit cream dessert.*

# CHICKEN LIVER AND CHIVE MASH PIES WITH ONION GRAVY

**SERVES 4**

6 rashers of streaky bacon
2 tablespoons sunflower oil
4 large shallots, finely chopped
1 garlic clove, crushed
15 g/½ oz butter
1 teaspoon fresh thyme leaves
325 g/12 oz chicken livers
salt and pepper

**Chive mash**
675 g/1½ lb floury potatoes,
    such as King Edwards, cut
    into large chunks
50 g/2 oz butter
25 g/1 oz Parmesan cheese,
    finely grated
2 tablespoons chopped chives

**Onion gravy**
1 tablespoon sunflower oil
1 small onion, finely chopped
1 carrot, finely chopped
50 g/2 oz mushrooms, sliced
1 bay leaf
1 sprig of thyme
few white peppercorns, crushed
300 ml/10 fl oz white wine
1 tablespoon redcurrant jelly
600 ml/1 pint chicken stock
300 ml/10 fl oz beef stock
3–4 tablespoons red onion
    marmalade (page 37)

For the onion gravy, heat the oil in a saucepan, add the vegetables, herbs and peppercorns and fry over high heat until deep golden. Add the wine and boil until reduced to a couple of tablespoons. Add the redcurrant jelly, chicken and beef stock and boil until reduced to 300 ml/10 fl oz. Strain into a clean pan and set aside.

For the chive mash, boil the potatoes until tender, drain, return to the pan and mash with the butter. Stir in the cheese and the chives and season to taste. Keep hot.

Preheat the grill to high. Cut each bacon rasher in half and grill until crisp. Finely chop four pieces and set aside. To cook the chicken livers, heat ½ tablespoon of the oil in a frying pan. Add the shallots, garlic, butter and thyme and fry until the shallots are soft. Tip into a bowl and keep hot. Wipe the frying pan and reheat it over high heat. Season the livers and add to the pan with the rest of the oil. Toss over high heat for about 1 minute until well browned on the outside but still moist in the centre. Tip into the bowl with the shallots, add the chopped bacon and mix well. Check the seasoning.

Add the onion marmalade to the gravy, bring to the boil and leave over a low heat. Place four lightly greased 10 cm/4 inch metal cutters on a greased baking sheet. Reheat the mashed potatoes, then spoon a layer into each cutter. Add the hot chicken livers and cover with the remaining potatoes. Slide the baking sheet under the hot grill for a few minutes, until the tops are golden. Slide a fish slice under each 'pie' and place on warmed plates. Remove the cutters and place two pieces of bacon on each pie. Spoon the gravy around the outside.

*Begin with crab soufflé. Serve hot chocolate soufflé as a finale.*

# SLOW-ROAST CHICKEN THIGHS
## with spicy couscous and apricot and mint sauce

**SERVES 4**

4 boned chicken thighs,
    about 125 g/4 oz each
salt and pepper
2 tablespoons olive oil
1 garlic clove, lightly crushed
1 tablespoon fresh lemon juice

**Couscous**
25 g/1 oz butter
1 teaspoon ground coriander
1 teaspoon ground cinnamon
½ teaspoon ground cumin
1 tablespoon soft brown sugar
375 ml/12 fl oz chicken stock
225 g/8 oz couscous
25 g/1 oz raisins
15 g/½ oz pine kernels, toasted
3 tablespoons olive oil
1 tablespoon fresh lemon juice
2 tablespoons chopped fresh mint

**Apricot and mint sauce**
25 g/1 oz butter
85 g/3 oz shallots, thinly sliced
1 garlic clove, crushed
1 teaspoon each of ground
    cinnamon and coriander
½ teaspoon each of ground
    cumin and turmeric
1 teaspoon light soft brown sugar
50 g/2 oz no-need-to-soak
    apricots, chopped
200 ml/7 fl oz chicken stock
1 tablespoon chopped fresh mint

For the sauce, melt the butter in a small saucepan. Add the shallots and garlic and fry gently for about 4 minutes or until soft. Add the spices and sugar and cook for 3 minutes. Add the apricots and stock, cover and simmer gently for 15 minutes. Add the chopped mint, then blend in a liquidizer or with a hand blender until smooth. If the sauce looks too thick, thin down with a little more stock. Check the seasoning and keep warm.

Season the chicken thighs well on both sides. Heat a frying pan over medium heat. Add the oil and garlic to the pan and then the chicken, skin-side down, and cook for about 20 minutes, until the skin is richly golden and very crisp. Turn the chicken over, discard the garlic and cook for another 2 minutes. Add the lemon juice and shake well to distribute it evenly. Cook for 3 minutes and then keep warm.

For the couscous, melt the butter in a large saucepan. Add the spices and fry gently for 1 minute. Add the sugar and stock and bring to the boil. Pour in the couscous in a steady stream, stir in the raisins and pine kernels and cover with a tight-fitting lid. Remove from the heat and set aside for about 6–8 minutes to allow the grains to swell up. Then uncover and fork in the olive oil, lemon juice, chopped mint and seasoning to taste.

To serve, carve each chicken thigh into six or seven pieces. Pile the couscous in the centre of four warmed plates, place the chicken on top and pour the sauce around the edge.

*Begin your dinner with a celery and tomato soup and finish with a simple crème caramel or light caramel mousse.*

# PAN-FRIED GUINEA FOWL
## *with a Mediterranean vegetable crumble*

**SERVES 4**

4 guinea fowl breasts, skin on
salt and pepper
1 tablespoon sunflower oil
15 g/½ oz butter
1 teaspoon fresh lemon juice
tapenade sauce (page 36)

**Vegetable crumbles**

1 small aubergine, cut into
    12 thin slices
1 red pepper
a little sunflower oil
1 large courgette, cut lengthways
    into four, then cut into
    1 cm/½ inch pieces
2 plum tomatoes, skinned,
    seeded and finely diced
1 tablespoon pesto
50 g/2 oz fresh white
    breadcrumbs
25 g/1 oz Parmesan cheese,
    finely grated
1 tablespoon olive oil

For the crumbles, layer the aubergine in a colander with a little salt and leave for 15 minutes. Rinse and leave to drain. Roast the red pepper over a gas flame or under a hot grill until black all over. Place in a plastic bag, seal and leave until cold, then peel off the skin, discard the seeds and cut the flesh into small pieces. Heat a frying pan until very hot. Add a little sunflower oil and the courgette and stir-fry for 2 minutes. Tip into a bowl and mix in the red pepper, tomatoes, pesto and seasoning. Heat a little more oil in the frying pan and fry the aubergine slices until well browned on both sides. Preheat the oven to 220°C/425°F/Gas Mark 7. Place four 10 cm/4 inch metal cutters on a lightly greased baking sheet. Place a slice of aubergine in each one, then half the courgette mixture, a slice of aubergine, the rest of the courgette mixture and top with aubergine. Mix together the breadcrumbs, Parmesan and olive oil. Season to taste and spread over the crumbles.

Season the guinea fowl. Heat a frying pan until very hot, add the oil and butter, then the guinea fowl, skin-side up, and cook for 2 minutes. Turn over and cook for 3–4 minutes, until the skin is well browned. Sprinkle with the lemon juice and transfer the pan to the oven, together with the crumbles. Cook the guinea fowl for 2 minutes, then remove, turn skin-side up and keep in a warm place for 10 minutes. Cook the crumbles for another 12–13 minutes, until golden brown.

Reheat the tapenade sauce. Slide a fish slice under each crumble, place on warmed plates and remove the cutters. Slice the guinea fowl and serve with the sauce.

*For a first course, scallops marinated in lime, honey and mint could be served with salad leaves. Finish with crème brûlée.*

# PHEASANT BREAST WITH SPINACH,
## *potato pancake and a mushroom velouté sauce*

**SERVES 4**

4 pheasant breasts, about
   150 g/5 oz each, skinned
salt and pepper
2 tablespoons sunflower oil
25 g/1 oz butter

**Wilted spinach**

1 tablespoon olive oil
1 small garlic clove, crushed
225 g/8 oz fresh spinach
   leaves, washed and large
   stalks removed
squeeze of lemon juice

**Mushroom and tarragon**
**velouté sauce**

300 ml/10 fl oz white wine
450 ml/15 fl oz game
   or chicken stock
150 ml/5 fl oz double cream
15 g/½ oz butter
175 g/6 oz mixed wild
   mushrooms, cleaned,
   stalks trimmed and sliced
1 tablespoon chopped fresh
   tarragon

**To serve**

potato pancakes (page 35)

For the sauce, put the white wine into a small saucepan and boil until reduced to a couple of tablespoons. Add the stock and boil until reduced by half. Add the cream, bring back to the boil, and simmer for a couple of minutes until it has acquired a good sauce consistency. Set aside and make the potato pancakes.

Season the pheasant breasts on both sides. Heat a large frying pan, add the oil and butter and when it is foaming, add the pheasant breasts and cook for 3–4 minutes on each side until nicely golden. Remove and keep warm.

To finish the sauce, reheat gently. Meanwhile, add the butter to the frying pan and as soon as it starts to foam, add the mushrooms and stir-fry over a high heat for 3–4 minutes until lightly browned. Stir them into the sauce together with the chopped tarragon, any juices from the pheasant and a little seasoning. Keep warm.

To cook the spinach, heat the olive oil in a large saucepan. Add the garlic, spinach and a little seasoning and stir-fry over a high heat until it has just wilted. Add the lemon juice and then drain in a colander.

To serve, place a potato pancake in the centre of four warmed plates and pile the spinach on top. Slice the pheasant breasts diagonally, rest them on top of the pancakes and spoon the mushroom sauce around the outside.

*For an autumn dinner you could begin with a warm salad of seared salmon and finish with an open fruit tart – cherries or pears in an almond base.*

# PIGEON BREASTS WITH ROAST BARLEY,
## *wild mushrooms and sauce vierge*

**SERVES 4**

8 pigeon breasts, skinned
2 tablespoons sunflower oil
25 g/1 oz butter
salt and pepper

**Roast barley with wild mushrooms**
3 tablespoons olive oil
175 g/6 oz pearl barley,
 washed and drained
1 small onion, very finely chopped
½ clove garlic, crushed
450 ml/15 fl oz chicken stock
2 tablespoons light soy sauce
150 ml/5 fl oz red wine
50 g/2 oz unsalted butter
225 g/8 oz wild mushrooms,
 cleaned, trimmed and
 sliced if large

**Sauce vierge**
200 ml/7 fl oz extra virgin
 olive oil
125 g/4 oz shallots, finely
 chopped
1 garlic clove, lightly crushed
1 sprig of thyme
1 bay leaf
2 tablespoons sherry vinegar

For the sauce vierge, put the oil, shallots, garlic, herbs, 1 teaspoon salt and 12 turns of pepper into a small pan and heat until just simmering. Cook very gently for about 20 minutes to soften the shallots, but not colour them. Remove from the heat, add the vinegar and set aside.

To cook the barley, heat a large frying pan until hot. Add the oil and barley and cook, stirring, until golden. Add the onion and garlic and cook for about 5–10 minutes until it starts to brown. Add the stock, soy sauce, wine and seasoning and simmer for about 10 minutes, until almost all the liquid has been absorbed. Meanwhile, heat another large frying pan until hot. Add 25 g/1 oz of the butter and the mushrooms and fry for a few minutes until lightly browned, then season. When the barley is ready, stir in the mushrooms, remove from the heat and cover loosely with foil. Pierce a few holes in the foil and set aside for about 15 minutes.

Season the pigeon breasts on both sides. Heat a large frying pan until hot, add the oil and butter and as soon as it is foaming, add the pigeon and cook for 2 minutes. Turn and cook for another minute, then remove from the heat and leave in a warm place to relax for 10 minutes.

To serve, remove the garlic, thyme and bay leaf from the sauce and warm through over a low heat. Stir the rest of the butter into the barley, check the seasoning and then spoon it into the centre of four warmed plates. Cut each pigeon breast in half, arrange on top of the barley and spoon some of the sauce around the outside.

*Begin your 'wild' menu with a pike mousseline, served with a tomato and chervil butter sauce. A classic lemon tart would conclude this flavoursome menu.*

# SEARED BREAST OF MALLARD
## *with savoury lentils*

**SERVES 4**

4 mallard breasts,
175 g/6 oz each
1 tablespoon sunflower oil
25 g/1 oz butter
sea salt and white pepper

**Savoury lentils**

175 g/6 oz dried Puy lentils
2 tablespoons olive oil
1 large shallot, finely chopped
1 small garlic clove, finely
chopped
1 small carrot, finely diced
1 small parsnip, finely diced
¼ swede, finely diced
250 ml/8 fl oz chicken stock
1 teaspoon chopped fresh
rosemary
1 teaspoon chopped fresh thyme
1 tablespoon chopped fresh
tarragon
2 tablespoons double cream
1 tablespoon softened butter

**To garnish**

deep-fried herbs (page 37)

Drop the lentils into a saucepan of lightly salted boiling water and simmer for 15–20 minutes or until just tender. Drain well and set aside.

Season the mallard on both sides. Heat a frying pan until hot, add the oil and butter and as soon as it is foaming, add the mallard, skin-side up, and cook for about 2 minutes. Turn and cook for a further 5–10 minutes, depending on how thick the breasts are and how pink you like your duck. Turn skin-side up and leave in a warm place to relax for 10 minutes.

To finish the lentils, heat the olive oil in a saucepan, add the shallot, garlic, carrot, parsnip and swede and cook for a few minutes, until soft. Add the cooked lentils, chicken stock, rosemary and thyme and simmer for 5 minutes. Add the tarragon, cream and butter and simmer for a further 2–3 minutes, by which time the lentils should have a loose sauce consistency – not too wet, not too dry. Stir in any juices from the duck and season to taste.

To serve, spoon the lentils into four warmed large soup plates. Carve the mallard breasts into slices, rest them on top and garnish with a pile of deep-fried herbs.

*Relax with a first course and pudding that you can prepare ahead. How about baby leeks vinaigrette with crisp Parmesan biscuits, then a soft chocolate cake with mascarpone cream and espresso coffee sauce?*

# Glazed duck skewers
## with Chinese greens and a soy, honey and ginger sauce

**SERVES 4**

4 duck breasts, 175 g/6 oz each
1 tablespoon Japanese soy sauce
1 tablespoon clear honey
juice of ½ lime
2 teaspoons Dijon mustard
1 tablespoon sunflower oil

**Stir-fried Chinese greens**
225 g/8 oz pak choi
   (Chinese cabbage)
1 tablespoon sunflower oil
few drops of sesame oil
1 garlic clove, very finely chopped
1 teaspoon Asian fish sauce
juice of ½ lime

**Soy, honey and ginger sauce**
2.5 cm/1 inch piece of fresh
   ginger
2 tablespoons Japanese
   soy sauce
2 tablespoons clear honey
1 tablespoon lime juice
1–2 teaspoons tomato purée
2 tablespoons dry sherry
250 ml/8 fl oz chicken stock
1 red chilli, seeded and very
   finely chopped

Remove the skin from the duck breasts and cut the meat into 2.5 cm/1 inch pieces. Mix together the soy sauce, honey, lime juice and mustard in a shallow dish. Add the duck and stir well to coat in the marinade. Set aside for 30 minutes.

Thread the pieces of duck on to eight 15 cm/6 inch bamboo skewers and set aside.

For the sauce, grate the ginger very finely and squeeze the juice into a small saucepan. Discard the remaining fibrous material. Add the remaining sauce ingredients to the pan and boil for 2–3 minutes until reduced to a thin sauce consistency. Set aside and keep warm.

For the stir-fried greens, slice the pak choi into 5 cm/ 2 inch pieces. Heat the sunflower and sesame oil in a wok or large saucepan, add the garlic and the pak choi and stir-fry over a high heat for 2–3 minutes, until just tender. Stir in the fish sauce and lime juice; keep warm.

Heat a ridged cast-iron griddle pan over high heat until hot. Reduce the heat, brush the pan with sunflower oil and then add the duck skewers and cook for a few minutes, turning occasionally, until the duck is browned on all sides but still moist and pink in the centre.

To serve, spoon the stir-fried greens into the centre of four warmed plates. Rest the skewers on top and spoon the sauce around the outside.

*Since this dish really needs no accompaniment, you might begin with a pasta course, say fettuccine with wild mushrooms. Continue the Oriental theme with a mango pudding – if you're feeling adventurous, try mango mousse with mango sauce.*

# ROAST SADDLE OF HARE
## with parsnip purée and a game and chocolate sauce

**SERVES 4**

8 loins of hare from 2 saddles;
  reserve the bones for
  the sauce
1 tablespoon sunflower oil
50 g/2 oz butter
sea salt and white pepper

**Parsnip purée**
450 g/1 lb parsnips,
  cut into chunks
600 ml/1 pint milk
50 g/2 oz butter

**Game and chocolate sauce**
1 carrot, roughly chopped
2 tablespoons sunflower oil
4 shallots or 1 small onion,
  chopped
50 g/2 oz mushrooms, sliced
2 bay leaves
2 sprigs of thyme
6 white peppercorns, crushed
300 ml/10 fl oz red wine
600 ml/1 pint chicken stock
300 ml/10 fl oz beef stock
50 g/2 oz blueberries
1 tablespoon crème de cassis
7 g/¼ oz bitter plain chocolate
15 g/½ oz butter

**To garnish**
deep-fried parsnips (page 37)

First make the sauce. Preheat the oven to its highest temperature. Chop the hare bones and spread in a roasting tin, together with the carrot. Roast for 20–30 minutes, until well browned. Heat the oil in a large saucepan, add the shallots, mushrooms, bay leaves, thyme and peppercorns and fry for a few minutes, until golden. Add the wine and boil until reduced to a couple of tablespoons. Add the roasted bones and both stocks and simmer for about 1 hour. Strain into another saucepan, leave to stand for a few minutes and then spoon off any fat from the surface. Bring back to the boil and boil until reduced to 300 ml/10 fl oz. Set aside.

For the parsnip purée, simmer the parsnips in the milk for 20–25 minutes, until very tender. Drain well. Purée the parsnips. The purée should be very thick; if necessary, return to a clean pan and cook, stirring, until the excess liquid has evaporated. Beat in the butter, season well and keep warm.

Season the hare. Heat a large frying pan until hot, add the oil and butter and fry the hare for 2–3 minutes on each side, until well browned. Leave in a warm place for about 10 minutes. Cook the deep-fried parsnips. Reheat the purée. Bring the sauce to a simmer, add the berries, crème de cassis and any juices from the hare. Cook until the berries are just tender. Spoon the parsnip purée on to four warmed plates. Slice the hare and arrange on the purée with the deep-fried parsnips on top. Whisk the chocolate and butter into the sauce and check the seasoning. Spoon some sauce over the meat and the rest, together with the blueberries, around the purée.

*Begin with tartare of salmon, perhaps with cucumber 'spaghetti'. Finish with a caramelized apple tart.*

# SLOW-ROAST HAUNCH OF VENISON
## with red cabbage and the best-ever roast potatoes

**SERVES 8**

3 kg/7 lb haunch of venison
   on the bone
12 garlic cloves, peeled
3 sprigs of rosemary,
   broken into small pieces
2 onions, quartered
300 ml/10 fl oz red wine
125 g/4 oz unsalted butter
salt and pepper

**Red cabbage**
50 g/2 oz butter
450 g/1 lb red cabbage,
   cored and thinly sliced
2 tablespoons redcurrant jelly
3 tablespoons sherry vinegar
finely grated zest and juice
   of 1 orange
125 ml/4 fl oz port
250 ml/8 fl oz red wine
85 g/3 oz raisins

**To serve**
best-ever roast potatoes
   (page 35)

Preheat the oven to 190°C/375°F/Gas Mark 5. Line a large roasting tin with foil, large enough to fold over and cover the venison. Scatter the garlic and rosemary over the venison and tuck in the onion quarters. Pour on the wine and season well. Melt the butter until foaming, pour over the venison and then bring the edges of the foil together and seal well. Place in the oven and roast for 3 hours.

For the red cabbage, melt the butter in a large saucepan. Add the cabbage and stir to coat in the butter. Add the redcurrant jelly and stir until it has melted. Add the vinegar, orange zest and juice, port, red wine and some seasoning. Bring to the boil and simmer for about 1 hour, until the cabbage is tender. Set aside for 1 hour.

Remove the venison from the oven and leave in a warm place to relax for about 40 minutes.

Increase the oven temperature to 240°C/475°F/Gas Mark 9 and roast the potatoes.

Meanwhile, stir the raisins into the cabbage, bring back to a simmer and cook gently for another 30 minutes.

To serve, unwrap the venison and lift on to a carving tray. Strain the juices into a small saucepan and check the seasoning. Carve the venison and serve with the cabbage and roast potatoes. Spoon some of the juices over the meat.

*Before this rich dish, serve a light starter such as trout fillet with avocado and sauce vierge (page 22). Afterwards, poached pears with a champagne syrup would slip down nicely.*

# MEDALLIONS OF VENISON
## with roasted root vegetables and a rich game sauce

**SERVES 4**

450 g/1 lb venison fillet,
  trimmed of fat and membrane
  (reserving the trimmings) and
  cut into 12 slices
2 tablespoons sunflower oil
4 small shallots, chopped
50 g/2 oz button mushrooms,
  sliced
½ garlic clove, crushed
1 bay leaf
1 sprig of thyme
6 white peppercorns, crushed
300 ml/10 fl oz red wine
1 teaspoon redcurrant jelly
600 ml/1 pint chicken stock
300 ml/10 fl oz beef stock
50 g/2 oz butter
1 tablespoon double cream

**Roasted root vegetables**
3 tablespoons sunflower oil
40 g/1½ oz butter
¼ swede, cut into 8 slices
2 large carrots, cut into 8 slices
4 sticks of celery, cut into
  5 cm/2 inch pieces
12 new potatoes, boiled until
  tender, drained and cut in half

**To garnish**
deep-fried thyme sprigs
  (page 37)

Lightly flatten the venison slices to about 1 cm/½ inch thick. Cover and set aside. Heat the oil in a large saucepan, add the meat trimmings and fry over a high heat until well browned. Add the shallots, mushrooms, garlic, bay leaf, thyme and peppercorns and fry until golden. Add the wine and boil until reduced to about 2 tablespoons. Add the redcurrant jelly, chicken and beef stock and boil until reduced to about 300 ml/10 fl oz.

For the roasted vegetables, preheat the oven to 230°C/450°F/Gas Mark 8. Heat 2 tablespoons of the oil and 25 g/1 oz of the butter in a cast-iron casserole dish. Add the swede, carrots and celery and fry for 5−6 minutes over a high heat, until well coloured. Season and add just enough water to cover the vegetables. Bring to the boil and reduce by two-thirds. Transfer to the oven and cook for about 12 minutes until the water has been absorbed and the vegetables are just tender. Meanwhile, heat the rest of the oil and butter in a frying pan, add the potatoes and fry, cut side down, for a few minutes until crisp and golden. Turn off the oven, leave the door ajar and leave the vegetables and potatoes inside.

Season the venison on both sides. Heat a large frying pan until very hot, add a little oil and 25 g/1 oz of the butter, then add half the medallions and fry for about 2 minutes on each side. Keep warm while you cook the rest. Bring the sauce back to a simmer and whisk in the remaining butter and the cream. Put the potatoes and vegetables in the centre of four warmed plates. Rest three medallions on the vegetables, spoon a little sauce over the meat and garnish with deep-fried thyme.

*For a winter feast, start with filo baskets of mussels with bacon and Brie; finish with Armagnac parfait with prunes.*

# The Basics

## CHICKEN STOCK

3 chicken carcasses
1 small head of garlic
1 large carrot, quartered
2 leeks, cleaned and sliced
2 sticks of celery, halved
1 onion, skin left on, quartered
6 white peppercorns
1 bay leaf
1 sprig of thyme
15 g/½ oz parsley stalks

Remove the skin and fat from the carcasses and place the carcasses in a very large pot. Add about 2.5 litres/4 pints cold water to just cover. Bring to the boil, skimming off any fat and scum as it rises. Cut the garlic in half horizontally. Lay the garlic and the rest of the ingredients on top of the carcasses, reduce the heat and leave to simmer very gently for 3–4 hours.

Strain the stock first through a colander and then through a fine sieve into a tall container. Leave in the refrigerator overnight.

Skim any fat off the surface and the stock is ready to use or freeze.

## BEEF STOCK

4.5 kg/10 lb beef knuckle bones
2 large carrots, cut into pieces
2 large onions, cut into wedges
2 large leeks, cut into pieces
2 sticks of celery, cut into pieces
1 head of garlic, halved
15 g/½ oz parsley stalks
1 bay leaf
1 large sprig of thyme
12 black peppercorns
3 plum tomatoes, quartered
2 tablespoons tomato purée
300 ml/10 fl oz red wine
1 pig's trotter
900 g/2 lb shin of beef

Preheat the oven to 200°C/400°F/Gas Mark 6. Place the bones in a large roasting tin and roast for about 1 hour until well browned.

Pour off the fat and reserve. Heat a very large pot, add 3 tablespoons of the reserved fat, then add the vegetables, garlic, herbs and peppercorns and stir over a high heat until well browned. Add the tomatoes and tomato purée and cook until the tomatoes have turned to a pulp. Add the wine and boil until reduced to a few tablespoons. Add the roasted bones, the pig's trotter and the shin of beef and cover with cold water. Bring to the boil, skimming the surface frequently. Reduce the heat and leave to simmer very gently for at least 8 hours and preferably overnight.

Strain the stock into a clean container and leave to cool. Skim off any fat and pour the liquid through a fine sieve. The stock is now ready to use or freeze.

## POTATO PANCAKES

325 g/12 oz floury potatoes,
    peeled and cut into chunks
2 tablespoons plain flour
2 tablespoons milk
2 tablespoons double cream
2 medium eggs, beaten
sunflower oil

Cook the potatoes in boiling salted water for 20 minutes or until soft. Drain well and then mash. Beat in the flour, milk, cream, eggs and seasoning to taste and then press the mixture through a sieve to remove any lumps. To cook, preheat the grill to high. Heat about 1 tablespoon of the sunflower oil in a 10 cm/4 inch blini pan. Add one quarter of the batter and cook over a high heat until the edge of the pancake begins to brown. Slide the pan on to the bottom shelf of the grill and cook for about 10 minutes, until the pancake is set and lightly browned on top. Flip over on to a baking sheet and keep warm while you make another three pancakes.

## BEST-EVER ROAST POTATOES

1.5 kg/3 lb large, floury
    potatoes, such as Cyprus,
    Golden Wonder or Kerr's
    Pink, peeled and cut in half
    only if very large
6 tablespoons sunflower oil

Preheat the oven to 240°C/475°F/Gas Mark 9. Put the potatoes in a saucepan of boiling salted water, bring back to the boil and boil for about 15 minutes, until almost fully cooked, but still a bit hard in the middle. Drain and leave in the colander for a few minutes. Pour the oil into a large roasting tin that will hold all the potatoes in one layer, with a little room to spare. Slide the tin into the top of the oven to allow the oil to get really hot. Return the potatoes to a dry pan, cover and shake to rough up the edges. Add the potatoes to the roasting tin and spoon some of the hot oil over each one (or turn them over in the oil) so that they all become well coated. If there's a lot of oil still left in the tin, drain it off. Return to the top of the oven and roast for about 40 minutes, turning them about every 10 minutes until crisp and golden all over.

## TAPENADE SAUCE

50 g/2 oz unsalted butter
2 shallots, thinly sliced
4 button mushrooms, sliced
1 bay leaf
1 sprig of thyme
300 ml/10 fl oz red wine
300 ml/10 fl oz chicken stock
200 ml/7 fl oz double cream

**Tapenade**

50 g/2 oz canned anchovy fillets
50 g/2 oz canned tuna in oil
50 g/2 oz dry salted capers
2 garlic cloves
175 g/6 oz pitted black olives
juice of ½ lemon
leaves from 1 sprig of thyme
1 fresh bay leaf
100 ml/3½ fl oz olive oil
1 tablespoon brandy

First make the tapenade. Drain the anchovies and tuna. Rinse the capers. Place all the ingredients in a food processor and blend for about 2 minutes, until smooth. Scrape the mixture into an airtight container and store in the refrigerator for up to 4 weeks.

To make the tapenade into a sauce, melt the butter in a saucepan. Add the shallots, mushrooms, bay leaf and thyme and fry for a few minutes, until golden. Add the wine and boil until reduced to about 2 tablespoons. Add the stock and boil until reduced by two-thirds. Stir in the cream and 1–2 tablespoons of the tapenade and bring the sauce back to the boil. Pour it through a sieve into a clean saucepan, pressing it through with the back of a ladle.

## Red onion marmalade

1.5 kg/3 lb red onions
85 ml/3 fl oz olive oil
100 ml/3½ fl oz sherry
  vinegar
2 tablespoons crème de
  cassis (optional)
salt and pepper

Slice the onions thinly. Heat the olive oil in a large, heavy-based frying pan. Add the onions and cook over a low heat, stirring occasionally, for 1½ hours, until the onions are very soft and richly caramelized. Add the sherry vinegar and simmer for a few more minutes, until thickened. Stir in the crème de cassis, if using, and season to taste.

## Deep-fried garnishes

Use the same principle to make crisp, colourful garnishes from thin slices of Parma ham, baby parsnips (cut them lengthways into four, blanch in boiling salted water for a few minutes until tender, then drain and dry well on paper towels) and herbs such as basil, dill, tarragon, flat-leaf parsley, thyme or chives.

Heat about 5–8 cm/2–3 inches of sunflower oil in a deep pan to 190°C/375°F, or until a cube of bread browns in 30 seconds.

Deep-fry the Parma ham, two slices at a time, for about 30 seconds, until crisp. Deep-fry the parsnips for a few minutes until crisp and golden. Drop in small handfuls of the herbs and deep-fry until the bubbling has subsided. Using a slotted spoon, lift out and drain on paper towels.

# Classic Cooking

STARTERS

**Lesley Waters** A former chef and now a popular television cook, appearing regularly on *Ready Steady Cook* and *Can't Cook Won't Cook*. Author of several cookery books.

VEGETABLE SOUPS

**Elisabeth Luard** Cookery writer for the *Sunday Telegraph Magazine* and author of *European Peasant Food* and *European Festival Food*, which won a Glenfiddich Award.

GOURMET SALADS

**Sonia Stevenson** The first woman chef in the UK to be awarded a Michelin star, at the Horn of Plenty in Devon. Author of *The Magic of Saucery* and *Fresh Ways with Fish*.

FISH AND SHELLFISH

**Gordon Ramsay** Chef/proprietor of London's Aubergine restaurant, recently awarded its second Michelin star, and author of Glenfiddich Award-winning *A Passion for Flavour*.

CHICKEN, DUCK AND GAME

**Nick Nairn** Chef/patron of Braeval restaurant near Aberfoyle in Scotland, whose BBC-TV series *Wild Harvest* was last summer's most successful cookery series, accompanied by a book.

LIVERS, SWEETBREADS AND KIDNEYS

**Simon Hopkinson** Former chef/patron at London's Bibendum restaurant, columnist and author of *Roast Chicken and Other Stories* and *The Prawn Cocktail Years*.

VEGETARIAN

**Rosamond Richardson** Author of several vegetarian titles, including *The Great Green Cookbook* and *Food from Green Places*.

PASTA

**Joy Davies** One of the creators of *BBC Good Food Magazine*, she has been food editor of *She, Woman* and *Options* and written for the *Guardian, Daily Telegraph* and *Harpers & Queen*.

CHEESE DISHES

**Rose Elliot** The UK's most successful vegetarian cookery writer and author of many books, including *Not Just a Load of Old Lentils* and *The Classic Vegetarian Cookbook*.

POTATO DISHES

**Patrick McDonald** Former chef/patron of the acclaimed Epicurean restaurant in Cheltenham, and food consultant to Sir Rocco Forte Hotels.

BISTRO

**Anne Willan** Founder and director of La Varenne Cookery School in Burgundy and West Virginia. Author of many books and a specialist in French cuisine.

ITALIAN

**Anna Del Conte** Author of several books on Italian food, including *The Gastronomy of Italy, Secrets from an Italian Kitchen* and *The Classic Food of Northern Italy* (chosen as the 1996 Guild of Food Writers Book of the Year).

## VIETNAMESE

**Nicole Routhier** One of the United States' most popular cookery writers, her books include *Cooking Under Wraps, Nicole Routhier's Fruit Cookbook* and the award-winning *The Foods of Vietnam*.

## MALAYSIAN

**Jill Dupleix** One of Australia's best known cookery writers and broadcasters, with columns in the *Sydney Morning Herald* and *Elle*. Her books include *New Food* and *Allegro al dente*.

## PEKING CUISINE

**Helen Chen** Author of *Chinese Home Cooking,* she learned to cook traditional Peking dishes from her mother, Joyce Chen, the *grande dame* of Chinese cooking in the United States.

## STIR-FRIES

**Kay Fairfax** A writer and broadcaster whose books include *100 Great Stir-fries, Homemade* and *The Australian Christmas Book*.

## NOODLES

**Terry Durack** Australia's most widely read restaurant critic and co-editor of the *Sydney Morning Herald Good Food Guide*. He is the author of *YUM*, a book of stories and recipes.

## NORTH INDIAN CURRIES

**Pat Chapman** Founded the Curry Club in 1982. A regular broadcaster on television and radio, he is the author of 20 books, which have sold more than 1 million copies.

## GRILLS AND BARBECUES

**Brian Turner** Chef/patron of Turner's in Knightsbridge and one of Britain's most popular food broadcasters; he appears frequently on *Ready Steady Cook, Food and Drink* and many other television programmes.

## SUMMER AND WINTER CASSEROLES

**Anton Edelmann** Maître Chef des Cuisines at the Savoy Hotel, London. Author of six cookery books, he has also appeared on television.

## TRADITIONAL PUDDINGS

**Tessa Bramley** Chef/patron of the acclaimed Old Vicarage restaurant in Ridgeway, Derbyshire and author of *The Instinctive Cook*.

## DECORATED CAKES

**Jane Asher** Author of several cookery books and a novel. She has also appeared in her own television series, *Jane Asher's Christmas* (1995).

## FAVOURITE CAKES

**Mary Berry** One of Britain's leading cookery writers, her numerous books include *Mary Berry's Ultimate Cake Book*. She has made many television and radio appearances.

## ICE CREAMS AND SEMI FREDDI

**Ann and Franco Taruschio** Owners of the renowned Walnut Tree Inn near Abergavenny in Wales, soon to appear in a television series, *Franco and Friends: Food from the Walnut Tree*. They have written three books together.

Text © Nick Nairn 1997

Nick Nairn has asserted his right to be identified
as the author of this Work.

Photographs © Philip Wilkins 1997

First published in 1997 by
George Weidenfeld & Nicolson
The Orion Publishing Group
Orion House
5 Upper St Martin's Lane
London WC2H 9EA

British Library Cataloguing-in-Publication data
A catalogue record for this book is available from
the British Library

ISBN 0 297 82284 5

Designed by Lucy Holmes
Edited by Maggie Ramsay
Food styling by Louise Pickford
Typesetting by Tiger Typeset